I KNOW That I AM

By Min. Teresa Taylor

About the Author

Meet Minister Teresa Taylor, a caring and compassionate individual whose journey is marked by faith, service, and creative expression. As an accomplished author of Christian books, journals and sermons, Teresa's words have touched hearts and guided souls on their spiritual paths. Her passion for spreading the message of love, hope, and redemption extends beyond the pages of her books and journals.

Teresa's dedication to her faith and obedience to God, led her to create the impactful online ministry, John 1:1 Ministry, found at www.john1OneMinistry.org. Through this platform, she reaches a global audience, inspiring individuals to deepen their relationship with God and embrace the teachings of Jesus Christ.

Beyond her ministry, Teresa is a devoted partner to her husband, Chad Taylor, sharing a life that's rooted in their shared faith. Together, they've created a nurturing homestead in the picturesque landscapes of North Carolina. It's here that they raise endearing fainting goats, cultivating a serene environment that mirrors the tranquility of their spiritual journey.

Her love for the land transcends into her vibrant garden, where she finds solace and inspiration. But Teresa's creative spirit doesn't stop there—she's an accomplished writer and painter, channeling her experiences and insights into artistic expressions that resonate deeply with others.

While her ministry and creative pursuits occupy her heart, family holds a special place. Teresa finds immense joy in spending time with her grandchildren, nieces, and nephew, cherishing the moments that create lasting bonds and memories.

Teresa's journey to ministry is an evolution rooted in her commitment to public service. Prior to embracing her calling to the ministry, she devoted herself to a career as a deputy sheriff and crime scene investigator. Her service-oriented heart and dedication to truth & justice laid the foundation for her life's work of guiding others toward spiritual fulfillment.

Armed with a bachelor's degree in social sciences from Gardner-Webb University, Teresa combines her academic foundation with her life experiences to deliver messages of empowerment, compassion, and transformation.

Minister Teresa Taylor is an embodiment of faith, service, and creativity. Her unwavering dedication to sharing God's love, both through her words and actions, shines as a beacon of hope and inspiration to all who cross her path.

I would like to dedicate this book to

God the Father, my Savior Jesus Christ, and His Holy Spirit

Table of Contents

Introduction ....pg. 5

Chapter One – Made in the Image of God ....pg. 7

Chapter Two – Treasured Above All ....pg. 10

Chapter Three – Known and Made for a Purpose ....pg. 13

Chapter Four – Precious and Loved ....pg. 16

Chapter Five – Born to Prosper ....pg. 19

Chapter Six – A Joy & Delight ....pg. 22

Chapter Seven - Chosen ....pg. 24

Chapter Eight – Saved from the Curse ....pg. 27

Chapter Nine – A New Person ....pg. 30

Chapter Ten – A Citizen of Heaven ....pg. 33

Chapter Eleven – A Royal Heir ....pg. 37

Chapter Twelve – A Member of a VIP Body ....pg. 40

Chapter Thirteen – Accepted ....pg. 43

Chapter Fourteen – Clean ....pg. 46

Chapter Fifteen – Heard ....pg. 49

Chapter Sixteen – Supernaturally Blessed ....pg. 52

Chapter Seventeen – Strong ....pg. 55

Chapter Eighteen – Complete ....pg. 59

Chapter Nineteen – More than a Conqueror pg.62

Chapter Twenty – Kept pg.65

Chapter Twenty-One – Inseparable ....pg. 68

Chapter Twenty-Two – I Know the Great I AM ....pg. 71

Chapter Twenty-Three – I Am His Story ....pg. 75

John 17 ....pg. 77

References ....pg. 80

Introduction

In the world today, unlike any other time in the history of the earth, there are so many people who do not know their own identity. So many are going through an identity crisis, identifying with other creatures and genders. There are so many mental health issues in every nation around the globe, and it is very heartbreaking. Because behind all these world issues and identity crisis' , there is a hurting broken heart, broken life and a soul who has wandered off the path that leads to their destiny and their purpose in life. The world is hurting terribly, and doesn't realize, they have a Father that feels their pain and has made a way for them to be whole. So much so, that He wanted me to stop my current assignment, to write this book, to remind every soul who reads it, of who they are, and how important they are to Him, through affirmations that He has given us in His Holy Word. Each chapter is from a scripture that He gave me, to remind you. So, if you are reading this now, it is not by accident. God is reaching out to you, to bring you healing, to mend your broken heart, to help you become confident of who YOU are and what YOU mean to Him.

After reading this book, please visit www.John1OneMinistry.org and reach out to me and testify of what God has done for you, so that the world may know of the goodness of God.

Thank you,

I love you,

And May God richly bless you.

Min. Teresa Taylor

"Then we who are alive and remain shall be caught up together with them in the clouds to meet the Lord in the air. And thus, we shall always be with the Lord. Therefore comfort one another with these words. ~ 1 Thessalonians 4:18

Dear Heavenly Father,

I pray for each and every one who has picked up this book, that Your Holy Spirit will guide them and give them wisdom, knowledge and understanding of the words and prayers that are written in this book. I pray that You will help them through their journey, direct their paths to know who You are and that by knowing You they may come to know more of themselves and who You made them to be. May they develop a deeper connection to You and may they be inspired to seek more of Your Holy Word. Father, I thank You for all who pick up this book, that it may be a source of inspiration, encouragement and transformation. Let Your truth resonates in their hearts. Bless each reader Father, with a renewed sense of purpose, an unwavering hope, and strengthen their love and faith in You. Let them come to know more of themselves and the intimate connection they have with Jesus Christ. Let them see how You are working in their lives and how You have never left them alone and abandoned. Father, I pray this book will be a help and a testimony of You, through all who pick it up. Thank You Father. In Jesus' Precious and Holy Name I pray.
Amen.

Chapter One

I KNOW that I AM

Made In the Image of God

~ Genesis 1:27

In the grand tapestry of creation, a profound revelation emerges: humanity is crafted in the image of God. Genesis 1:27 captures this extraordinary truth, declaring, "So God created man in His own image; in the image of God, He created him; male and female He created them." This chapter embarks on a journey to unravel the depth of this divine reality, exploring how our creation in God's likeness shapes our identity, purpose, and relationship with the Creator.

At the core of this 'Divine Likeness' resides the reflection of God's divine attributes in human nature. Our intellect, emotions, creativity, and capacity for relationships stand as distinct marks that mirror the essence of the Creator. While the full extent of God's being eludes our comprehension, the image we bear resonates with the core of the divine.

Genesis 1:28 further illuminates the concept of the 'Divine Likeness,' affirming, "God blessed them and said to them, 'Be fruitful and multiply; fill the earth and subdue it; have dominion over the fish of the sea, over the birds of the air, and over every living thing that moves on the earth.'" This dominion underscores humanity's role as stewards of creation. Just as God holds sovereignty over the cosmos, we are entrusted with the sacred responsibility to nurture and care for the earth, reflecting His dominion through our actions.

The Triune God — Father, Son, and Holy Spirit — exists in perfect unity and love. Likewise, we are body, mind and spirit, and are inherently wired for relationships, mirroring the divine community. Our capacity for love, empathy, and companionship finds its origin in the divine nature. Through our relationships, we tangibly express the love that characterizes God's being.

Embedded within the 'Divine Likeness' is our moral consciousness. Reflecting God's inherent goodness, we possess an intuitive sense of right and wrong. Moreover, our freedom to choose, to exercise free will, mirrors God's sovereignty over His creation. Our choices mirror the divine ability to make decisions and shape our path.

Although sin marred the 'Divine Likeness' within us, it was never obliterated. Through Christ's redeeming work, we find restoration. Colossians 3:10 prompts us to "put on the new self, which is being renewed in knowledge according to the image of its Creator." As we journey with Jesus Christ, we are transformed into His likeness, realizing our true identity in Him.

The 'Divine Likeness' transcends abstract concept; it defines our essence. We bear the likeness of God, encompassing attributes that mirror His character, dominion, relationships, morality, and free will. Our creation in God's image underscores our intrinsic worth and purpose, urging us to harmonize with our divine identity. Embracing this truth, we are compelled to honor God in our thoughts, actions, and relationships, allowing His light to radiate through us, illuminating a world yearning for restoration.

What does being created in His image tell you about yourself? _____

_____

_____

_____

What does being created in His image tell you about Him? _____

_____

_____

_____

Does knowing this change the way you see your past, present or future? _____

_____

How can knowing that you were created in His image make a difference in your life?

_____

_____

Something to think about:

Can you imagine what the image of God looks like? Look in the mirror. God has the same features that you do: Head, hair, eyes, ears, nose, mouth, a torso, arms, legs, hands, feet, fingers and toes. And when He came in the flesh in Jesus, YES, He DOES have a belly button!

Dear Heavenly Father,

I praise You and thank You for all Your goodness. I thank You that You would create me in Your image. I am but a speck of dust, compared to all that You are. You are Divine and Holy. I am lowly and sinful. Yet, I have Your attributes born into me, because You are my Father and I am Your child. I know that because of sin, I was born into this world to die, because that is the wages for the sin against You. I know You made all of creation perfect, without sin, without sickness or disease and certainly without death. But the enemy caused us to doubt You and sin against You. Even so, You already had a plan to redeem us back to You, through Your Son, Jesus, who is that part of You, who You sent int the flesh. He paid the penalty for my sin, so that at that appointed time, when He comes back to raise us up from the grave and renew our flesh to the original perfect condition that You intended from the beginning, undoing the works of the enemy that has brought death to all the world. Until then, Father, allow Your Holy Spirit to work in me, guiding me and teaching me more about You and more about who You made me to be. Show me who You made me to be. When I look in the mirror, let me see more of You. When other people look at me, let them see more of You. Let my life reflect whose child I really am. Thank you Father.

In Jesus Precious and Holy Name, Amen.

Chapter Two

I KNOW that I AM

Treasured Above All

~ Exodus 19:5

In a world filled with ever-changing standards of worth, it is a remarkable truth that each of us is treasured above all. Exodus 19:5 speaks to this truth, as God tells His people, "Now therefore, if you will indeed obey My voice and keep My covenant, then you shall be a special treasure to Me above all people." This chapter embarks on a journey to explore the depths of our treasured identity in God, supported by additional scriptures that affirm our unique worth.

Exodus 19:5 unveils the heart of God's intent for His people—to be a special treasure above all. This divine declaration echoes through the ages, signifying that we are not a result of mere chance, but a product of God's intentional design. Psalm 139:14 beautifully reaffirms this truth: "I praise you because I am fearfully and wonderfully made; your works are wonderful; I know that full well." Our uniqueness is a testament to God's exquisite craftsmanship.

Isaiah 43:1 further solidifies our treasured status: "But now, thus says the Lord, who created you, O Jacob, and He who formed you, O Israel: 'Fear not, for I have redeemed you; I have called you by your name; You are Mine.'" God's choosing is not haphazard; it is for a purpose. Just as He addressed Israel, He addresses each of us by name, signifying a personal relationship and a divine mission. Our lives are infused with purpose because we are treasured in His sight.

The New Testament echoes this sentiment, highlighting our priceless value in Jesus Christ. 1 Corinthians 6:20 declares, "For you were bought at a price; therefore, glorify God in your body and in your spirit, which are God's." The sacrifice of Christ on the cross underscores the incomparable worth God places on us. We are no longer bound by the world's estimation of value; we are redeemed by the precious blood of Jesus.

Romans 8:17 reminds us of our identity as children of God: "And if children, then heirs—heirs of God and joint heirs with Christ, if indeed we suffer with Him, that we may also be glorified together." As heirs of God's kingdom, we inherit a legacy of eternal significance. Our treasured identity encompasses a promise of co-glorification with Jesus Christ Himself.

In conclusion, Exodus 19:5 serves as a resounding declaration of our identity as treasures in God's eyes. Our worth is not determined by fleeting standards, but by the Creator who formed us with intentionality and love. As we journey through life, let us remember that we are chosen, purposed, redeemed, and heirs of the King. Let this truth empower us to live in the fullness of our treasured identity, shining as beacons of God's love and grace in a world hungering for a sense of worth.

You may not 'feel' treasured, but God says that you are. Do you think that He wants you to know your worth? _____

What has God done to show you how much you are worth to Him? _____

_____

Knowing that God treasures you, what are some ways that you can treat yourself better?

_____

_____

How does being treasured make a difference in your life? _____

_____

Knowing that each of us are treasures to God, how can that change the way we treat others?

_____

_____

_____

Something to think about:

Think of what you treasure most. Now think about all the treasures in the world. Can you imagine the unknown treasures in Heaven? Now realize that You are treasured ABOVE ALL OF IT!

Dear Heavenly Father,

Your works are wonderful, and I thank You for all of Your wonderful works of creation, from the sun and the moon and all the good things on this earth. I thank You Father for creating me and for giving me Your Word, to remind me that You treasure me above all the wonderful things You have made. Help me Father to remember my value to You, and to help me see others the way that You do. In times when others say or do things to me that make me feel worthless, remind me Father of the truths that You say about me. I love You and thank You. In Jesus' Precious and Holy Name. Amen

www.freepik.com Image by jcomp on Freepik

Chapter Three

I KNOW that I AM

Known and Made for a Purpose

~ Psalms 139:1, 13-16

In the tapestry of our existence, there lies a truth that surpasses all understanding: we are known and purposefully made. Psalm 139 captures this truth with poetic elegance, inviting us to explore the depths of our identity and the intentionality of our creation. This chapter embarks on a journey through Psalm 139:1, 13-16, illuminating the profound reality that we are not mere accidents, but intricately woven beings designed for a purpose.

Psalm 139:1 opens with a declaration of God's intimate knowledge: "O Lord, you have searched me and known me." The Psalmist acknowledges that every facet of their being, every hidden thought, and every unspoken word is fully known by God. This realization invites us to embrace the awe-inspiring truth that we are not anonymous or overlooked; we are known on the deepest level by our Creator.

Verses 13-16 delve into the remarkable process of our formation: "For you formed my inward parts; you knitted me together in my mother's womb. I praise you, for I am fearfully and wonderfully made. Wonderful are your works; my soul knows it very well. My frame was not hidden from you, when I was being made in secret, intricately woven in the depths of the earth. Your eyes saw my unformed substance; in your book were written, every one of them, the days that were formed for me, when as yet there was none of them."

These verses unveil the intricate craftsmanship of God in our creation. We are not random products of chance, but masterpieces formed with meticulous care. Our intricate design speaks to the divine intentionality behind our existence. From the secret place of our mother's womb to the very blueprint of our days, God's handiwork is evident.

Embedded within our creation is a unique purpose that aligns with God's divine plan. The Psalmist's acknowledgment of being "fearfully and wonderfully made" attests to the truth that we are designed with precision for a distinct purpose. This purpose is not determined by societal standards or personal aspirations alone; it is woven into the fabric of our being by the One who knows us intimately.

In conclusion, Psalm 139:1, 13-16 invites us into the sanctuary of divine intimacy and purposeful creation. We are known beyond measure, intricately formed in the secret chambers of our mother's womb. Our lives are not mere accidents; they are purposefully crafted by the hands of our Creator.

As we navigate life's journey, let us anchor ourselves in the truth that we are known by the One who intricately designed us. Our purpose is not an elusive concept; it is a reality intricately woven into our existence. May this realization empower us to walk boldly in our identity, embracing the divine design that shapes our lives and propels us toward the destiny God has ordained for us.

The Psalmist said that God has searched you and has known you. Do you remember searching for something? How important was it to you? _____

Have you ever studied something that you were interested in? When he said that God searched and has known you, we can deduct that God studied you intrinsically. He knows us better than we know ourselves. What does that tell us about God's love for us? _____

_____

Something to think about:

God has paid very close attention to every detail on a cellular level, not only in us, but also in our lives. Psalm 139:16 says that God wrought us from the lowest parts of the earth, that He saw our substance, and wrote each part down AS HE WAS FORMING IT IN HIS MIND, before it was formed. This verse attests to His divine design of our individual creation, how much attention to every detail that He gave to us BEFORE He brought us into existence. God has known you, much longer than you have been alive. There is no friend and no one who has known you longer than Him. And if you want to be known by others, you must be who God made you to be, Yourself.

Dear Heavenly Father,

In your wisdom You saw all my substance and even wrote them down before You formed me. I know that when You made me in Your image, You had a purpose for my life. Father as I learn more about You and more about myself, please help me to see all the attributes that You have given me, to know my purpose. Father, God, it is so good to know that You know me better than I know myself and that You have known me longer than anyone. I know you created me for a purpose, even though I cant always see it, or know what that purpose is, I do know that with the help of Your Holy Spirit, I can know that all of the experiences in my life, and all the lessons I have learned, all the interests and gifts that You have given me, will be revealed at the right time and make sense to me at the right time and that my life will be devoted to the purpose You made me for. I give You my life Father, to do Your good pleasure and will. And I thank You, that I was not an accident and that You have not abandoned me, that you have known me. I thank you for giving my life meaning and purpose. In Jesus' Precious and Holy Name I pray. Amen

Chapter Four

I KNOW that I AM

Precious and Loved

~ Isaiah 43:4

In a world that often measures worth by external standards, there exists a truth that transcends all human understanding: we are precious and loved. Isaiah 43:4 shines as a radiant gem amidst the Scriptures, declaring, "Since you are precious and honored in my sight, and because I love you, I will give people in exchange for you, nations in exchange for your life." This chapter embarks on a journey through the depths of Isaiah 43:4, supported by other Scriptures that affirm our inherent worth and the unbreakable love bestowed upon us.

Isaiah 43:4 stands as a divine proclamation of our value: "Since you are precious and honored in my sight." In these words, God unveils His heart toward us. Our worth is not determined by our achievements, appearance, or societal status; it is etched within the very fabric of our being by the Creator Himself. This declaration resonates through eternity, affirming that we are treasures held dear in God's gaze.

Romans 8:38-39 reinforces the unbreakable nature of God's love: "For I am convinced that neither death nor life, neither angels nor demons, neither the present nor the future, nor any powers, neither height nor depth, nor anything else in all creation, will be able to separate us from the love of God that is in Christ Jesus our Lord." This profound truth underscores that God's love for us knows no bounds. It's a love that defies circumstances and transcends every obstacle.

1 John 3:1 tenderly affirms our identity as beloved children of God: "See what great love the Father has lavished on us, that we should be called children of God! And that is what we are!" As children of God, we are cherished members of His family. This love bestowed upon us is not based on our performance but is an outpouring of His nature.

John 3:16 encapsulates the ultimate sacrifice of love: "For God so loved the world that he gave his one and only Son, that whoever believes in him shall not perish but have eternal life." The magnitude of God's love is revealed through the sacrifice of Jesus Christ. This sacrificial act demonstrates the depths to which God values and loves us.

In conclusion, Isaiah 43:4 echoes through the corridors of time, reminding us that we are precious and loved in the sight of our Creator. This truth liberates us from the constraints of human opinions and societal expectations. We are enveloped in a love that is unshakable, unbreakable, and unwavering—a love that surpasses all understanding.

As we journey through life, let us remember that our identity is rooted in God's declaration of our preciousness and the outpouring of His unending love. This truth empowers us to walk confidently, secure in the knowledge that we are treasured by the One who gave everything for us. May this reality shape our perspective, our relationships, and our actions as we radiate the love that we have received from the heart of our Heavenly Father.

We have all had our days where someone says something about us or to us that makes us feel discouraged and worthless. But who are they compared to God? And why should their opinion carry more weight than His truth? What has made you feel worthless? _____

_____

Now, considering what God says about us, is what made you feel worthless true? _____

If it is not true, then how can you stop feeling and acting as if it were? _____

_____

Something to think about:

Not only does God say that we are precious to Him, but He honors us! To be honored by the greatest and highest power is amazing! People can be honored by their family, school, even the President of the United States; but no higher honor can you receive than that from God! Maybe we do not feel we deserve it, but that is how God rolls, because it isn't about what we think, but what HE thinks.

Dear Heavenly Father,

How great is Your unending love! You Father are Love and I thank you for loving me so much. Your love not only tells me how much I mean to You, but it teaches me how great You are. I know that all love flows from You. It makes no earthly sense to me, that You would send Your Only Son, Jesus, to die on the cross for my sins. I know I am not worthy of your love, for all the mistakes and failures and sins that I have committed against You, yet You still love me and call me precious in Your sight. I thank You that love, especially the love You showed at the cross, the love that was poured out through the precious blood, covers all my sins and faults. And I am so blessed that nothing I could do can separate or take away the love You have for me. When I feel unlovable, and I feel that I have let You down, let me take heart and repent, and thank you for Your love, because it is those times that teach me how great You are. Father, let nothing come between us, and I pray that my love grows deeper and stronger for You each day, and help me to love others the way that You do. In Jesus' Precious and Holy Name, Amen.

Chapter Five

I KNOW that I AM

Born to Prosper

~ Jeremiah 29:11

In the midst of life's uncertainties, there is a promise that shines as a beacon of hope: we are born to prosper. Jeremiah 29:11 declares, "For I know the plans I have for you, declares the Lord, plans for welfare and not for evil, to give you a future and a hope." This chapter embarks on a journey to explore the depth of Jeremiah 29:11, supported by other Scriptures that reinforce the divine assurance of a prosperous destiny.

Jeremiah 29:11 stands as a divine assurance of a promising future: "For I know the plans I have for you, declares the Lord, plans for welfare and not for evil, to give you a future and a hope." In these words, God unveils His heart toward us. Our destiny is not a result of mere chance or circumstance; it is intricately woven into God's plan for our lives. This declaration resounds throughout history, affirming that prosperity is woven into the fabric of our existence.

John 10:10 echoes the promise of abundant life through Jesus Christ: "The thief comes only to steal and kill and destroy; I have come that they may have life and have it to the full." Jesus' mission is to bestow life in all its fullness upon us. This abundant life encompasses not just material blessings, but spiritual abundance, purpose, and fulfillment.

3 John 1:2 reinforces the comprehensive nature of prosperity: "Beloved, I pray that all may go well with you and that you may be in good health, as it goes well with your soul." The apostle John's prayer for prosperity extends to our well-being in every aspect of life—physical, emotional, and spiritual. This prayer echoes God's heart for our holistic prosperity.

Malachi 3:10 illustrates the concept of prosperity through the principle of tithing: "Bring the full tithe into the storehouse, that there may be food in my house. And thereby put me to the test, says the Lord of hosts, if I will not open the windows of heaven for you and pour down for you a blessing until there is no more need." God's promise of prosperity includes the principle of abundant blessings when we align with His ways.

In conclusion, Jeremiah 29:11 shines as a resounding promise of divine prosperity. Our future is not marred by uncertainty or despair; it is intricately designed by the hands of our Heavenly Father. As we navigate the journey of life, let us anchor ourselves in the truth that we are born to prosper in the embrace of God's plan.

This promise empowers us to live with confidence, trusting that our destiny is secure in God's loving hands. Divine prosperity encompasses not only material blessings but also spiritual abundance, purpose, and fulfillment. May this truth infuse us with hope, courage, and a resolute commitment to walk in the prosperity that God has ordained for us.

Remember being a young child and all the crazy things you pretended to be or tried to do? Children have a hard time accepting that there is something that they can't have or something that they can't do? They know that they were born to prosper, with all their needs met, they have not a care in the world. How has God met your needs? _____

_____

What has kept you from prospering, not just financially, or socially, or physically, but in every aspect of life? _____

_____

_____

And what does God say about it? _____

_____

_____

Something to think about:

Jesus said to consider the sparrows, how they neither work nor toil and yet God provides for them. And then He asked, "Are you not worth more than two sparrows?" Do you realize that humans are the only species on this planet with a currency that we must pay to live here? That is the wicked way of the world, and not a part of God's plan. God does not need money to care and provide for us. He can prosper us in every way, when we trust in Him and allow His will to be done. Money does not control Him but can control us if we let it. Live in God's will, not money's control.

Dear Heavenly Father,

You hold all blessings and riches and glory. I know that Your will for me is to prosper in every way. And I know that through You, with the help of the Holy Spirit, I will prosper spiritually, physically, financially. I thank You that Your Word is truth and through the truth You have given me, I know I have a future, hope, assurance and that I am safe and secure in You. I know that if there is anything I ask, in Your Name, believing, you will give it to me. I know that You are working ALL things for my good, for Your Glory. Help me to prosper in the fruits of my labor, and in a way that is pleasing to you. Help me prosper according to Your will, in everything, that others may see Your Goodness and that You may be glorified. Whenever I begin to worry about my finances, my future, my relationships, remind me Father to have faith in You and always remember Your plans for my good and prosperity. Father, keep me in good health, that I may continue to do your will. Bless me, that I may be a blessing to others. My cup runneth over in abundance and prosperity, thanks to You, my God. You more than meet all my needs. I cannot thank You enough, and there are not enough words, all I can say is thank You. In Jesus' Precious and Holy Name, Amen.

www.freepik.com Image by jcomp on Freepik

Chapter Six

I KNOW that I AM

A Joy & Delight

~ Zephaniah 3:17

In a world often shrouded in negativity and turmoil, there exists a truth that radiates like a beacon of light: we are a joy and delight. Zephaniah 3:17 resonates with this truth, declaring, "The Lord your God is in your midst, a mighty one who will save; he will rejoice over you with gladness; he will quiet you by his love; he will exult over you with loud singing." These words paint a vivid picture of God's heart toward us. We are not overlooked or unimportant; we are cherished and celebrated by the Creator Himself. This declaration echoes throughout eternity, affirming that we bring joy to the heart of God. This chapter embarks on a journey through the profound assurance of Zephaniah 3:17, supported by other Scriptures that affirm our status as God's joy and delight.

Psalm 149:4 affirms God's delight in the righteous: "For the Lord takes pleasure in his people; he adorns the humble with salvation." The Psalmist declares that God takes pleasure in His people. This pleasure is not conditional on our achievements or performance; it is a response to our relationship with Him. Our humility and salvation adorn us as recipients of His delight.

Proverbs 17:6 underscores the joy that children bring: "Grandchildren are the crown of the aged, and the glory of children is their fathers." Just as the joy of grandchildren uplifts the elderly, our relationship with God brings delight to Him. We are His children, and our existence brings glory to the Father's heart.

Luke 15:7 reveals the joy that accompanies repentance: "Just so, I tell you, there will be more joy in heaven over one sinner who repents than over ninety-nine righteous persons who need no repentance." The act of repentance brings joy not only to the individual but also to the heart of God and the heavenly realm. Our decision to turn toward God's embrace fills His heart with delight.

In conclusion, Zephaniah 3:17 resounds as a divine symphony of joy and delight. We are not insignificant or unnoticed; we are embraced by the One who rejoices over us with gladness. This truth empowers us to rise above the challenges of life, anchored in the knowledge that we are cherished by our Heavenly Father.

This realization transforms our perspective, infusing our lives with joy and purpose. We are not defined by circumstances or opinions; we are defined by the One who delights in us. As we journey through life, let us carry the melody of divine joy and delight, radiating the love that we have received from the heart of our Creator.

Happiness and Joy are two different things. Happiness is fleeting, it comes and goes. But Joy is a substance that lasts. You can be sad, scared, angry and yet still be filled with a joy that surpasses every emotion. Think back through all the years of your life. Can you remember times when you were filled with joy? _____

_____

_____

You are the apple of God's eye. You bring Him Joy and you are His delight. Who in your life do you delight in, who brings you Joy? _____

_____

Now, do they have to do anything for you to feel that way about them? _____

_____

Something to think about:

Where there is joy, the Holy Spirit is there. You cannot be filled with joy apart from Him. Ultimately, He is the source of all Joy, just as you, being His creation are the source of His joy.

Dear Heavenly Father,

I thank You that You have made it known to me that I am Your Joy and Delight. I thank you for the Joy that you fill my life with as well. As long as you love and cherish me, I can go about my day with Joy and Purpose, knowing that Your opinion of me is the only one that matters. Father, when I think about that all of heaven rejoiced at my salvation, with singing and gladness, let me not be puffed up, that I am so loved. But fill me with Your Joy and I pray that I can keep that love and joy and spread it wherever I go. I want to share You with others. I think about how different this world I live in would be, if only we were all filled with Your joy. I cannot even imagine what heaven must be like. I pray that my actions not only delight, but Glorify You Thank you, Father. In Jesus' Precious and Holy Name. Amen

Chapter Seven

I KNOW that I AM

Chosen

~ John 1:12, 15:11,16

In a world that often grapples with feelings of insignificance, a profound truth emerges: we are chosen. John 1:12, 15:11, and 15:16 speak to this exquisite reality, declaring that we are not merely spectators in God's story; we are cherished participants, intentionally chosen to be part of His divine narrative. This chapter embarks on a journey through these verses, bolstered by other Scriptures that celebrate our chosen status.

John 1:12 illuminates our adoption as children of God: "But to all who did receive him, who believed in his name, he gave the right to become children of God." This verse underscores the privilege of being chosen. We are not left as strangers; we are embraced as family members in the house of God. This status reflects the heart of the Father who longs for a relationship with us.

John 15:11 emphasizes the joy derived from abiding in Jesus Christ: "These things I have spoken to you, that my joy may be in you, and that your joy may be full." As chosen ones who abide in Christ, we partake in His joy. Our chosenness isn't rooted in duty or obligation; it is rooted in a relationship that fills our lives with abundant joy.

John 15:16 reinforces our appointed purpose: "You did not choose me, but I chose you and appointed you that you should go and bear fruit and that your fruit should abide, so that whatever you ask the Father in my name, he may give it to you." This verse echoes our chosen role in God's kingdom. We are appointed to bear lasting fruit—fruit that transforms lives and glorifies God.

Ephesians 1:4-5 reaffirms our chosen status and purpose: "For he chose us in him before the creation of the world to be holy and blameless in his sight. In love he predestined us for adoption to sonship through Jesus Christ, in accordance with his pleasure and will." God's choice wasn't arbitrary; it was preordained before the foundations of the world. We are chosen to reflect His holiness and grace.

In conclusion, John 1:12, 15:11, and 15:16 stand as divine declarations of our chosen status. We are not random wanderers; we are purposefully selected by the Creator of the universe. Our lives are not accidental; they are marked by intentionality and divine purpose.

As we navigate the journey of life, let us walk as the chosen ones—embracing our identity as children of God, delighting in the joy of abiding in Christ, and bearing fruit that glorifies Him. Our chosenness empowers us to live with confidence and purpose, secure in the knowledge that we are cherished by the One who chose us. May this truth radiate through our lives, inviting others to experience the transformative embrace of God's choice.

Do you carefully and considerately choose your friends, or the people who you allow to be a part of your life? _____

There are many things that we do not choose, and there are times when we wish we had chosen differently. When we choose something or someone, it is not random, but carefully considered. Can you remember a time when you were in school and were waiting to be chosen for something? How does it feel, to know that God chose you before the foundations of the earth were made?
_____

Knowing that God has chosen you, that you were not an accident or born out of random, how does that change or influence the decisions that you will make in your life? _____

_____

_____

Something to think about:

Regardless of your faith, you were chosen and belong to God. Jesus said, "you did not choose me, I chose you". Sure, when Jesus asked the disciples to follow Him, they had a choice, and He will not go against their free will. But they had the opportunity to make that decision only because He first chose them. God chose you before the heavens and earth were created, regardless of if you choose Him or not, HE CHOSE YOU.

Dear Heavenly Father,

You are Holy and have chosen me before the foundations of the earth were laid. I come to You in humility, knowing that on my own, I could never bear the fruit that would bring You glory. And knowing all my mistakes, it's hard for me to see myself as chosen by You. But through Your Word, that is Truth, I know that, if I believe You sent Jesus to die for me, that I am Your Child. I am a child of the Most High God who created me, and that You will help me. Help me find the divine purpose that you created me for. I know that my life is not an accident, for you intended me and created me for a purpose. I pray your Holy Spirit, leads and guides me, to bring forth the fruit that You have Chosen me to bare, to help me see the importance and responsibility of being a member of Your Family, to reflect Your love and Your Kingdom, for all to see You. I thank You Father, that as Your child, I can ask you anything. I thank you for allowing me to partake of Your Joy. I pray that I grow closer and closer to You and who You say that I am. In Jesus' Precious and Holy Name. Amen.

_____

_____

_____

_____

_____

_____

_____

_____

_____

_____

_____

Chapter Eight

I KNOW that I AM

Saved From the Curse

~ Galatians 3:13

In a world burdened by the weight of sin and its consequences, a liberating truth emerges: we are saved from the curse. Galatians 3:13 proclaims, "Christ redeemed us from the curse of the law by becoming a curse for us, for it is written: 'Cursed is everyone who is hung on a pole.'" This chapter embarks on a journey through this powerful declaration, reinforced by additional Scriptures that illuminate the profound nature of our salvation from the curse.

Galatians 3:13 unveils the redemptive work of Christ: "Christ redeemed us from the curse of the law by becoming a curse for us." These words encapsulate the heart of the Gospel—the sacrificial love of Jesus, who willingly took upon Himself the curse that rightfully belonged to us. This act of divine exchange marked the end of our bondage to sin's curse and inaugurated our freedom.

Romans 6:6-7 reinforces our liberation from sin's dominion: "For we know that our old self was crucified with him so that the body ruled by sin might be done away with, that we should no longer be slaves to sin—because anyone who has died has been set free from sin." Through Christ's redemptive act, we are no longer slaves to sin's curse. We are set free to walk in the newness of life.

1 Corinthians 15:55-57 proclaims our triumph over death: "Where, O death, is your victory? Where, O death, is your sting? The sting of death is sin, and the power of sin is the law. But thanks be to God! He gives us the victory through our Lord Jesus Christ." Through Christ's curse-bearing sacrifice, we have gained victory over death itself. The curse's hold is shattered, replaced by the promise of eternal life.

Galatians 5:1 celebrates our freedom in Christ: "It is for freedom that Christ has set us free. Stand firm, then, and do not let yourselves be burdened again by a yoke of slavery." As recipients of Christ's redemptive work, we are liberated from the curse's chains. Our lives are marked by the freedom to live in the fullness of God's grace and purpose.

In conclusion, Galatians 3:13 stands as a triumphant declaration of our salvation from the curse through Christ's redemptive sacrifice. Our lives are no longer defined by the curse of sin; they are defined by the victory of the Cross. We are liberated to live as children of God, walking in the freedom that Christ secured for us.

As we journey through life, let us embrace our identity as those saved from the curse. Let us stand firm in the victory of Christ, empowered to overcome sin's grip and live in the fullness of redemption. May the transformative power of this truth radiate through our lives, inviting others to experience the life-changing embrace of Christ's salvation.

The very first law that was given, was for our benefit, to keep us safe, when God told Adam, "Do not eat from that tree, for if you do, you will surely die." When Adam disobeyed the one and only law that was given him, he sinned, and the wages of that sin brought the penalty and curse of death upon everything and everyone in the whole earth. It doesn't matter if you feel that you are a good person. You were born to die. But God sent Jesus, to bare the curse on the cross for you, to pay the penalty of sin for you, so that you too could be saved and raised from the grave to have eternal life. Do you believe this? _____

Have you repented of your sins and asked Jesus to be Lord of your life, have you thanked Him for saving you from the curse?_____
_____

Do you realize there is nothing that you can do to save yourself from the curse of death? _____

Something to think about:

In the Old Testament, there was a divine curse placed on a person who was hung on a tree. Most crimes in those days that were punishable by death, the person was stoned to death. But in serious offenses, the person put to death was hung on a tree as a public deterrent to that crime. God said, 'cursed is the man who is hung on a tree'. When He spoke this divine curse, He knew that His only Son, Jesus, who was sinless, innocent and Holy, would in the future, be hung on a cross, cursed, for our sakes, to show how serious it is to sin against Him, as well as how serious He is about His love for us. When we die, we will not all be hung on a tree, because Jesus did that for us.

Dear Heavenly Father,

I praise Your Holy Name, the Name in which every knee shall bow, and every tongue confess that Jesus Christ is Lord! Thank You for the victory that Jesus did on the cross, to pay the penalty of my sin, to take upon Himself the curse of death and hell that I was under. I am so grateful and thankful that You wanted me to have eternal life with You, that You love me that much that You died for me, went to hell for me and took the keys to death and hell. Father, thank You for Your resurrection power that brought Jesus out of the grave and raised Him in the flesh to Your right hand, giving me the hope and promise of eternal life with You in Heaven. Even though my flesh will die, I know that You removed the curse of death from me and that one day You will raise me from the grave, as my Savior did. Help me to always be mindful of this. You also have the power and will to remove all curses from my life that the enemy tries to place on me. I thank You for the freedom from curses that You have given me. Thank You for Your loving protection and for Your life-giving resurrection! Knowing this truth, I can journey through my life, with newness and confidence. Through Your Holy Spirit, help me guard my mind, hold fast to my faith in You, and keep my eyes on You. Father, through Your Holy Spirit, help me to see opportunities to share this truth, Your Truth and Love with others in the world who so desperately need You. Help me to serve those in need and let them know that no matter what they are going through, that You love them and died for them and that they do not have to remain under the curse of death, that they too have eternal life through their faith in Jesus Christ. In His Precious and Holy Name. Amen.

Image By Studio Multiverse www.stock.adobe.com

Chapter Nine

I KNOW that I AM

A New Person

~ 2 Corinthians 5:17

In a world that often clings to the old, a transformative truth emerges: we are new creations. 2 Corinthians 5:17 declares, "Therefore, if anyone is in Christ, the new creation has come: The old has gone, the new is here!" This chapter embarks on a journey through this profound declaration, bolstered by additional Scriptures that illuminate the transformative nature of our new identity in Christ.

2 Corinthians 5:17 unveils the radical transformation we experience in Christ: "Therefore, if anyone is in Christ, the new creation has come: The old has gone, the new is here!" In these words, we are invited to recognize that our identity is no longer bound to the old patterns of sin and brokenness. Through Christ's work, we are reborn into a new reality—a reality of restoration, purpose, and wholeness.

Romans 12:2 speaks to the renewal of our minds: "Do not conform to the pattern of this world, but be transformed by the renewing of your mind. Then you will be able to test and approve what God's will is—his good, pleasing and perfect will." Our transformation is not merely external; it begins within the recesses of our minds. As new creations, our thought patterns align with God's truth and purpose.

Ephesians 4:22-24 speaks of shedding the old self and embracing the new: "You were taught, with regard to your former way of life, to put off your old self, which is being corrupted by its deceitful desires; to be made new in the attitude of your minds; and to put on the new self, created to be like God in true righteousness and holiness." As new creations, we actively participate in shedding the old self and clothing ourselves with the attributes of our new identity.

John 3:5-6 highlights our spiritual rebirth: "Jesus answered, 'Very truly I tell you, no one can enter the kingdom of God unless they are born of water and the Spirit. Flesh gives birth to flesh, but the Spirit gives birth to spirit.'" Through our faith in Christ, we are born anew by the Spirit. This rebirth marks the beginning of our journey as new creations in Christ.

In conclusion, 2 Corinthians 5:17 heralds the truth of our identity as new creations. The old has passed away, replaced by the newness of life in Christ. Our transformation extends beyond a mere change in behavior; it encompasses a complete shift in our essence and purpose.

As we navigate the paths of life, let us walk in the truth of our new identity. Let us embrace the reality that we are no longer defined by our past but by our future in Christ. May this truth empower us to live in the fullness of our calling as new creations, radiating the transformative power of Christ to a world in need of renewal.

In what ways have you become a 'New Creation' in Jesus Christ? _____
_____
_____

Have you noticed anything different in your daily life? _____
_____
_____

Being born again in the Spirit, you now can see things from a spiritual perspective and may notice supernatural things. Take note of any supernatural or miracles that you witness. How do you think God's Holy Spirit is directing you? _____
_____

Jesus said, 'my sheep hear my voice, and they know me'. Have you heard and recognized His voice? _____
_____

Something to think about:

Being a 'new creation', you now have direct access to talk with God and hear His voice because you can now see things from a spiritual perspective, and His Holy Spirit lives inside you. The Spirit never dies. You are a spirit, not just a mortal being, but a spiritual being. You are immortal. The spiritual becomes more real to you than the physical, knowing that everything that can be seen in the physical would not exist had it not been created first in the spiritual, that the physical is a direct manifestation of the spirit. Realizing your immortality is like the past, present and future all wrapped into one. You can see the past differently and not be bound to the past hurts and experiences that brought you to the present. You can live in the present with a new perspective. You can look forward to the future with surety, knowing what awaits you and knowing that there is nothing that you must face alone, no battle ahead that hasn't already been won. In the end, you win! Thank you, Jesus!

Dear Heavenly Father,

I come before You with a heart overflowing with gratitude and awe. Thank You for the precious gift of new life through Your Son, Jesus Christ. Through His sacrifice, I am reborn, transformed into a new creation, and embraced by Your unending grace. Father, I am humbled by the love You have poured into my life. You have washed away my past mistakes, and my sins, and You have granted me a fresh start. In this newness, I find hope and purpose. You have set my feet on a path of righteousness, guiding me with Your Holy Spirit. I praise You for the incredible journey You've led me on. You have opened my eyes to a new perspective—one rooted in Your truth, grace, and love. Your Word is a lamp to my feet and a light to my path, guiding me through each step of this newfound life. Thank You, Heavenly Father, for empowering me with Your Holy Spirit. You strengthen me, comfort me, and remind me of Your promises. I am not alone on this journey; Your presence is my constant companion. Through Your Holy Spirit, I am equipped to walk in a way that honors You, reflecting Your character to the world around me. Father may my life be a living testimony of Your transformative power. Help me to shine Your light in every corner of my existence. As I navigate this new life, I pray that others may see Your love, kindness, and grace through me. May my actions, words, and choices reflect Your heart. I surrender my life to You, Heavenly Father. Mold me, guide me, and shape me into the person You created me to be. I am forever grateful for Your mercy, Your forgiveness, and the unending love that You shower upon me. In Jesus' Precious and Holy Name. Amen.

Chapter Ten

I KNOW that I AM

A Citizen of Heaven

~ Philippians 3:20

In a world often divided by borders and nations, a profound truth emerges: we are citizens of heaven. Philippians 3:20 declares, "But our citizenship is in heaven. And we eagerly await a Savior from there, the Lord Jesus Christ." This chapter takes you on a journey through the significance of this heavenly citizenship, supported by additional Scriptures that illuminate the rich tapestry of our identity as citizens of heaven.

Philippians 3:20 reveals our true homeland: "But our citizenship is in heaven." In this declaration, we are reminded that this world is not our ultimate home. Our true citizenship lies in the eternal realms of heaven, where we are citizens of the kingdom of God. This truth transcends earthly borders and affiliations, anchoring us in an unshakable identity.

Philippians 3:20 speaks of our anticipation for our Savior's return: "And we eagerly await a Savior from there, the Lord Jesus Christ." As citizens of heaven, our hearts are stirred with hope as we eagerly anticipate the return of our Savior, Jesus Christ. This anticipation shapes our perspective, reminding us that our ultimate destiny is in His hands.

2 Corinthians 5:20 portrays us as ambassadors for Christ: "We are therefore Christ's ambassadors, as though God were making his appeal through us. We implore you on Christ's behalf: Repent of your sins, believe on the Lord Jesus Christ and be reconciled to God!" As citizens of heaven, we bear the responsibility of representing the heavenly kingdom on Earth. Our lives serve as testimonies of the kingdom's values, inviting others into the fold of God's grace.

Hebrews 11:13-16 describes us as pilgrims and strangers on Earth: "All these people were still living by faith when they died. They did not receive the things promised; they only saw them and welcomed them from a distance, admitting that they were foreigners and strangers on earth." This passage underscores that while we reside on Earth, our true identity as citizens of heaven makes us foreigners, pilgrims on a journey home.

In conclusion, Philippians 3:20 resonates as a clarion call to embrace our identity as citizens of heaven. While we reside on Earth, our true allegiance lies in the eternal realm. Our lives are marked by a heavenly perspective, an eager anticipation for Christ's return, and the responsibility of representing the kingdom of God.

As we journey through life, let us walk in the awareness of our heavenly citizenship. Let us shine as ambassadors of Christ, bearing witness to the values of our heavenly homeland. May this truth infuse our lives with purpose, hope, and an unshakeable assurance that we are citizens of the most glorious kingdom—the kingdom of heaven.

As a citizen of Heaven, how can you represent God's kingdom to those here on earth? _____

_____

_____

Knowing that you are a citizen of Heaven, how does that change how you see things in this world? _____

_____

_____

Make a chart with one side, the things of the world, the other side the things of Heaven. Notice the things that are different and the things that are the same and decide what conclusions you see. How do those conclusions align with what is written in God's Holy Word? _____

_____

_____

_____

Example:

The World	Heaven
Money	No need for money
Flowers	Flowers
Unseen, unknown angels	Angels seen and known

Something to think about:

Jesus bridged the gap for believers between Heaven and Earth. He is the way, the truth and life everlasting. This world is not our home. If we are citizens of Heaven, doesn't that make us foreign aliens on earth? If you were traveling to a different nation, how would you treat it while you are there?

Image By David https://stock.adobe.com/contributor/209328267/david?load_type=author&prev_url=detail

Dear Heavenly Father,

I praise You, Holy Father God, and I lift up my thanksgiving to You for the precious privilege of being a citizen of Your eternal Kingdom. Amid earthly challenges, I find solace in knowing that my true home resides in the embrace of Your Heavenly realm. As an ambassador of Your Kingdom, guide me to live out my heavenly citizenship in ways that honor YOU, reflecting the beauty of Your Kingdom's values. As I journey onward, may my life be a testament to Your love, grace and the hope that Your Kingdom offers to all who believe in my Lord Jesus Christ as the Savior Who died on the cross for their sins, arose from the grave and ascended to heaven, to reconcile us back to our true home with You. In Jesus Precious and Holy Name. Amen.

Chapter Eleven

I KNOW that I AM

A Royal Heir

~ Galatians 4:7

In a world that often measures worth by worldly standards, a profound truth illuminates our true identity: we are royal heirs. Galatians 4:7 proclaims, "So you are no longer a slave, but God's child; and since you are his child, God has made you also an heir." This chapter invites you to journey through the significance of our royal heritage, supported by Scriptures that unveil the depth of our identity as cherished and destined heirs.

Galatians 4:7 unveils our dual identity: "So you are no longer a slave, but God's child; and since you are his child, God has made you also an heir." In these words, we embrace our identity as God's children—loved, valued, and cherished. Beyond that, we stand as heirs, bestowed with an inheritance that transcends earthly riches—a divine inheritance that unfolds beyond measure.

Romans 8:17 proclaims our status as co-heirs with Christ: "Now if we are children, then we are heirs—heirs of God and co-heirs with Christ, if indeed we share in his sufferings in order that we may also share in his glory." As royal heirs, we are linked with Christ Himself. Our inheritance is intertwined with His, and our destiny is aligned with His glory.

Ephesians 3:6 reveals our connection to the promise: "This mystery is that through the gospel the Gentiles are heirs together with Israel, members together of one body, and sharers together in the promise in Christ Jesus." Our royal heritage extends to the promise of salvation. We are heirs who partake in the blessings and promises of the Gospel—a promise that bridges nations and generations.

Colossians 1:12 speaks of our inheritance in the saints: "giving thanks to the Father, who has qualified you to share in the inheritance of his holy people in the kingdom of light." Our royal heritage is intertwined with the community of saints. We are beneficiaries of a collective inheritance that spans across believers, uniting us in God's redemptive plan.

In conclusion, Galatians 4:7 resonates as a resounding affirmation of our identity as royal heirs. We are not confined by the limitations of this world; we belong to a heavenly lineage that spans eternity. Our identity as God's children and co-heirs with Christ empowers us to walk with purpose, hope, and the assurance that we are destined for greatness.

As we journey through life, let us embrace the truth of our royal heritage. Let us live in the fullness of our identity as beloved heirs of the King, carrying the responsibility to reflect His grace, love, and truth in a world hungry for purpose. May this truth shape our perspective and actions, radiating the majestic inheritance we carry as royal heirs.

How does it make you feel to be a royal heir to the throne of God? What does that mean to you?

_____

_____

_____

Knowing that we are heirs to the throne of God, what do you think of when you see poverty?

_____

_____

What can you do, or how can you help to change the poverty you see? _____

_____

_____

Something to think about:

All the goodness of God belongs to you, all that is in heaven and earth IS YOURS! No earthly king can top that! But remember, with great position comes great responsibility and with great responsibility comes great sacrifice. Jesus proved that.

Dear Heavenly Father,

I bow before Your majestic throne with a heart filled with awe and reverence. You are my King of Kings and my Lord of Lords, reigning in majesty and unmatched power. I am humbled by Your sovereignty and overwhelmed by Your love. Thank You, Father, for choosing me as Your child and making me a royal heir in Your Kingdom. What a privilege it is to be part of Your divine family, to share in the inheritance of Your grace and love. As a child of the King, I stand in awe of the riches and blessings that You lavish upon me. You rule your Kingdom in love, truth, justice and righteousness! How great You are! I praise You! With every breath, I praise Your name, O Lord. I celebrate Your unending goodness, Your unwavering faithfulness, and Your boundless mercy. Help me to carry the identity of a royal heir with honor, embracing the responsibility to reflect Your character in every aspect of my life. I find comfort and strength in knowing that I belong to You. May my actions and words exemplify the love and grace of Your Kingdom! May I walk confidently as a child of the King, spreading Your light wherever I go. Thank You, Heavenly Father, for the immeasurable privilege of being part of Your royal lineage, for adopting me and grafting me into Your vine. You are my Master! Your love has raised me to a position of a beautifully humble honor, and I am forever grateful for Your unchanging grace. In Your Majesty Jesus' Precious and Holy Name. Amen.

Image By Sketchepedia | Source www.freepik.com

Chapter Twelve

I KNOW that I AM

A Member of a VIP Body

~ 1 Corinthians 3:23, 12:27

In a world that often seeks exclusivity and distinction, a powerful truth emerges; we are members of the VIP body of Christ. 1 Corinthians 3:23 proclaims, "You are of Christ, and Christ is of God," while 1 Corinthians 12:27 affirms, "Now you are the body of Christ, and each one of you is a part of it." This chapter invites you to journey through the significance of being part of this VIP body, supported by Scriptures that reveal the profound connection we have as members of Jesus Christ's body.

1 Corinthians 3:23 underscores our unity with Jesus Christ: "You are of Christ, and Christ is of God." These words affirm our belongingness to Christ, highlighting the intimate connection we share with Him. We are not mere spectators or distant admirers; we are intimately united with Jesus Christ in a relationship that defines our very essence.

1 Corinthians 12:27 emphasizes our integration into the body of Jesus Christ: "Now you are the body of Christ, and each one of you is a part of it." As members of His body, we are integral components of the body of Christ. Each one of us contributes to the body's function and purpose, creating a harmonious symphony of diverse gifts, talents, and callings.

Romans 12:4-5 highlights the diversity within the body of Jesus Christ: "For just as each of us has one body with many members, and these members do not all have the same function, so in Christ we, though many, form one body, and each member belongs to all the others." Our membership transcends individualism; we belong to one another. Each member's uniqueness enriches the collective whole, fostering unity amidst diversity.

1 Corinthians 12:21-22 speaks to the importance of every member: "The eye cannot say to the hand, 'I don't need you!' And the head cannot say to the feet, 'I don't need you!' On the contrary, those parts of the body that seem to be weaker are indispensable." Every member, regardless of perceived prominence, holds vital significance in the body. Our contributions, however small they may seem, are indispensable.

In conclusion, 1 Corinthians 3:23 and 12:27 echo as invitations to embrace our identity as members of the VIP body of Jesus Christ. We are not isolated entities; we are intricately woven into a divine tapestry of unity, purpose, and community.

As we journey through life, let us walk in the consciousness of our membership in the body of Jesus Christ. Let us honor the uniqueness of each member, cherishing the unity that transcends boundaries and differences. May this truth inspire us to live as VIP members, carrying the responsibility to reflect Jesus Christ's love, grace, and unity to a world longing for authentic community.

As a member of the body of Jesus Christ, what do you think your function is? _____
_____

All the members of our body each have their own purpose but work together. How can you work together with other members of the body of Jesus Christ? _____
_____
_____

What do you think God wants us to accomplish being a part of Jesus' body? _____
_____

Something to think about:

Jesus is the Word of God. John 1:1 says, "In the beginning was the Word and the Word was with God and the Word was God...". Jesus came to earth in the flesh and is God. You are a part of HIM, being a member of His body. You were with Him, in His Heart and on His Mind when He hung on the cross. You were there. You are a part of His body. And He is a part of yours. Could there be any greater intimacy and connection to God than that? Realizing this, how will you treat your body?

Dear Heavenly Father,

I come before You with a heart overflowing with gratitude. Thank You Holy God for the honor of connecting me with the body of my Lord and King, Jesus Christ. Thank You for the intimate relationship and connection that I have with Him and my fellow believers. King Jesus, You are the head of this body and I am in awe of Your wisdom, grace and leadership, going before me to make my paths straight. Thank You for choosing me to be set apart for Your divine purpose. Help me to learn and carry out the responsibility of being a member of Your body, help me to know my role in being a member of this spiritual family. Thank You for uniting me with my fellow believers and for the relationships that transcends earthly boundaries. Help me to know my significance and be a powerful force for Your Kingdom. Help me to love, support, uplift and encourage my brothers and sisters in You, as we journey together in our faith and service to You King Jesus. May I never take for granted the privilege and honor of being a part of Your body. Help me, through Your Holy Spirit, to recognize the gifts and talents that You have given me, and to use them to do Your will that You may be glorified. I will wait on You, Holy Spirit, to show me what I can do for You and lead me in my actions and words to always bring honor and glory to the Father. I pray that You remove anything in me and my life that keeps me from You, and that keeps me from bringing You honor and glory. Keep me and never let me go, never let me stray from You, guard my heart and keep it abiding in You. Be with me always King Jesus. I love you with all that I am, and I am a part of You and You are a part of me. Move me and use me God for Your glory. You are my rock and I love You and trust You, forever. Holy, Holy, Holy are You God. In Jesus' Precious and Holy Name. Amen.

_____

_____

_____

_____

_____

_____

_____

_____

_____

Chapter Thirteen

I KNOW that I AM

Accepted

~ Romans 15:17

In a world that often measures worth by standards of achievement, a profound truth emerges: we are fully accepted. Romans 15:7 declares, "Accept one another, then, just as Christ accepted you, in order to bring praise to God." This chapter invites you to explore the significance of acceptance, grounded in the acceptance we receive from Jesus Christ, and supported by Scriptures that reveal the depth of our identity as beloved and fully accepted individuals.

Romans 15:7 highlights Christ's acceptance of us: "Accept one another, then, just as Christ accepted you." This verse underscores Christ's all-encompassing love and acceptance of us. He doesn't love us based on performance or achievement; His acceptance is grounded in His unchanging nature and grace. As we receive His acceptance, we are called to extend the same acceptance to others.

Romans 5:8 portrays God's unconditional love: "But God demonstrates his own love for us in this: While we were still sinners, Christ died for us." God's love isn't contingent on our perfection; it's rooted in His nature. He loved us when we were undeserving, highlighting the depth of His acceptance toward us.

Ephesians 1:4-5 reveals our chosen and adopted status: "For he chose us in him before the creation of the world to be holy and blameless in his sight. In love he predestined us for adoption to sonship through Jesus Christ, in accordance with his pleasure and will." God's acceptance of us is tied to His choosing and adopting us as His beloved children. This identity is based on His love and sovereignty.

Colossians 1:21-22 speaks of reconciliation through Jesus Christ: "Once you were alienated from God and were enemies in your minds because of your evil behavior. But now he has reconciled you by Christ's physical body through death to present you holy in his sight, without blemish and free from accusation." Through Jesus Christ, we have been reconciled to God. His acceptance removes the stain of sin, presenting us blameless in His sight.

In conclusion, Romans 15:7 resonates as a call to embrace our acceptance—both from Jesus Christ and toward one another. We are accepted by the Creator of the universe, not based on our merits, but on His boundless love and grace.

As we journey through life, let us live in the assurance of our acceptance. Let us extend this acceptance to others, fostering a culture of love and grace. May this truth empower us to walk confidently, knowing that we are fully accepted by the One who matters most—our Savior and Redeemer, Jesus Christ.

What are the reasons that you might feel unacceptable to God? _____
_____
_____

Knowing that you are covered by the blood of Jesus, do you realize that God does not see those things that you stated above. He saw those things before He even created you, but He loved you and created you anyway, with a plan to redeem you back to Him. He tells us to humble ourselves in order to come before Him. He accepted us, just as we are. What are the truths about you that you need to accept in order to humble yourself before God? _____
_____
_____

Knowing that God accepted you long before you were born, does that inspire you to want to change things about you for the better? What changes can you make in your life that would be pleasing to Him? _____
_____
_____

Something to think about:

By God accepting us, just as we are, He has given us the freedom to make mistakes from which we learn and grow.

Dear Heavenly Father,

I come before You with a heart full of gratitude for Your unwavering acceptance. Long before I took my first breath, You knew me and loved me. Your acceptance of me is a gift beyond measure, a reflection of Your boundless grace. Lord, as I bask in Your acceptance, help me to extend the same to others. Teach me to see people through Your eyes, recognizing the beauty of Your creation within them. Guide me to separate their sins from the precious souls You crafted. Empower me, Father, to live a life that is pleasing in Your sight. May my thoughts, words, and actions align with Your will, reflecting the gratitude I feel for Your acceptance of me. Give me the strength to follow in the footsteps of Your Son, Jesus Christ, who showed acceptance and love to all. In this world, may I stand as a beacon of Your unconditional acceptance. Help me to embrace others as they are, just as You embrace me. Grant me the wisdom to discern between sin and the essence of Your creation, that I may love without conditions. Thank You, Father, for accepting me before I even knew You. May Your acceptance be the foundation of my interactions, and may Your love shine through me to touch the lives of others.

Chapter Fourteen

I KNOW that I AM

Clean

~ 1 John 1:9

In a world often burdened by mistakes and guilt, a liberating truth emerges: we are cleansed and renewed. 1 John 1:9 proclaims, "If we confess our sins, he is faithful and just and will forgive us our sins and purify us from all unrighteousness." This chapter invites you to explore the profound significance of spiritual cleansing, supported by Scriptures that illuminate the depth of our identity as those who are forgiven and made new.

1 John 1:9 unveils the assurance of forgiveness and cleansing: "If we confess our sins, he is faithful and just and will forgive us our sins and purify us from all unrighteousness." These words resonate as a promise that no matter the depth of our mistakes, God's grace extends to cleanse and renew us. The act of confession initiates a process of restoration that transcends guilt and shame.

Hebrews 9:14 speaks of the cleansing power of Christ's blood: "How much more, then, will the blood of Christ, who through the eternal Spirit offered himself unblemished to God, cleanse our consciences from acts that lead to death, so that we may serve the living God!" Christ's sacrifice carries the power to cleanse our consciences from the stain of sin, allowing us to serve God with hearts made whole.

Titus 3:5 emphasizes our renewal through the Holy Spirit: "He saved us, not because of righteous things we had done, but because of his mercy. He saved us through the washing of rebirth and renewal by the Holy Spirit." Our spiritual cleansing and renewal are not the result of our own efforts, but rather the work of God's mercy and the transformative power of the Holy Spirit.

Isaiah 1:18 paints a picture of our sins being made white as snow: "Come now, let us settle the matter. Though your sins are like scarlet, they shall be as white as snow; though they are red as crimson, they shall be like wool." God's forgiveness transforms the deepest stains of sin into purity. Our sins, once scarlet, are made white through His redeeming grace.

In conclusion, 1 John 1:9 resounds as an invitation to embrace our identity as those who are cleansed and renewed through Christ's forgiveness. Our sins are not a permanent mark on our lives; they are steppingstones toward God's transformative grace.

As we navigate life's journey, let us walk in the assurance of our cleansing. Let us lay aside guilt and shame, embracing the truth that we are washed clean by the blood of Christ. May this truth empower us to live in the fullness of our identity, renewed and purified to serve the living God with hearts made whole.

When you take a bath or shower, how do you feel when you step out? _____
_____

When Jesus cleansed you from your sins, how did that feel? Was it similar to the feeling you get when you step out of the shower? Did you feel refreshed, renewed, rejuvenated? Do you feel new? _____
_____

What has that newness inspired you to do in your life? _____
_____

Something to think about:

When Jesus died on the cross, blood and water flowed from His side. Water is important to God. From it, He brought forth life, and cleansed the world of sin. Before Jesus began His ministry, He was baptized in water. God planted seed in the garden in Eden, and then He sent it water to make it grow. Before He came to earth, and before the Priests could come to Him, they had to cleanse themselves three times in water. They did not realize it, but they were cleansing once for the Father, once for the Son and once for the Holy Spirit. Cleanliness is Godliness.

Dear Heavenly Father,

Thank You for the forgiveness You offer through the sacrifice of Your Son, Jesus Christ. Help me to walk in the light of Your truth, free from the weight of guilt and shame. Guide me to make choices that honor Your holiness and reflect the beauty of a clean heart. As I seek Your cleansing, may Your Spirit work within me, transforming me into a vessel fit for Your purpose. Let me radiate the purity that comes from a life surrendered to You. Help me to be clean in every area of my life. May my thoughts, words, and actions be a testimony to Your redeeming power. Thank You for the promise of cleansing and renewal. I trust in Your mercy and grace, knowing that You can make me clean, inside and out. In Jesus' Precious and Holy Name. Amen

Image By Sketchepedia | Source: www.freepik.com

~ Isaiah 1:18

"…Though your sins are like scarlet, They shall be as white as snow…"

Chapter Fifteen

I KNOW that I AM

Heard

~ 1 John 5:14-15

In a world where voices often go unheard, a comforting truth emerges: we are heard by the Creator of the universe. 1 John 5:14-15 assures us, "This is the confidence we have in approaching God: that if we ask anything according to his will, he hears us. And if we know that he hears us—whatever we ask—we know that we have what we asked of him." This chapter invites you to explore the profound significance of being heard and understood by God, supported by Scriptures that illuminate the depth of our identity as those who approach the Almighty with confidence.

1 John 5:14 establishes our confidence in approaching God: "This is the confidence we have in approaching God: that if we ask anything according to his will, he hears us." The veil between humanity and divinity has been torn, granting us access to the very presence of God. As we approach Him, we do so with the confidence that our petitions are not in vain but are heard by the One who knows and cares for us intimately.

Luke 18:1-8 speaks to the power of persistent prayer: "Then Jesus told his disciples a parable to show them that they should always pray and not give up." This passage reinforces the truth that our prayers are heard even when answers don't come immediately. Persistence in prayer demonstrates our trust in God's sovereignty and His timing, knowing that He hears our heartfelt cries.

Matthew 7:11 highlights God's heart as a Father who listens: "If you, then, though you are evil, know how to give good gifts to your children, how much more will your Father in heaven give good gifts to those who ask him!" God, as our loving Father, delights in granting our requests. Just as earthly parents listen to their children's pleas, our heavenly Father listens with an even greater depth of compassion and understanding.

Romans 8:26-27 speaks of the Holy Spirit interceding for us: "In the same way, the Spirit helps us in our weakness. We do not know what we ought to pray for, but the Spirit himself intercedes for us through wordless groans." Even when our words fail us, the Holy Spirit intercedes on our behalf, conveying the deepest longings of our hearts to God.

In conclusion, 1 John 5:14-15 resonates as a reminder of our identity as those who are heard by the Almighty. Our prayers are not mere echoes in the void; they are heard by the One who holds the universe in His hands.

As we journey through life, let us walk in the assurance of being heard. Let us approach God with confidence, knowing that our petitions are received by the One who listens, understands, and responds in accordance with His perfect will. May this truth empower us to pray with boldness, trusting that the God who hears us is also the God who answers with wisdom and love.

When have there been times in your life, when it was obvious that God heard your prayer?

_____

_____

When have there been times in your life that you felt that no one heard you? _____

_____

_____

Have you ever been in company with someone, and you did not have to speak to be heard, but could understand in silence? _____

_____

Something to think about:

God listens with compassion and understanding. God hears you even when you are silent and have no words. Sometimes, in silence is when we can hear Him best.

Dear Heavenly Father,

I come before You with a heart brimming with gratitude. Thank You for hearing me, even when my words fail me. You understand the whispers of my heart, the unspoken burdens I carry, and the depths of my soul that long for Your presence. Lord, I'm thankful for the gift of prayer that Jesus bestowed upon us. He taught us to come to You as a loving Father who eagerly listens to His children. In times of joy, sorrow, confusion, and celebration, You incline Your ear to our cries. Thank You for promising that our prayers are heard. Your Word assures us that even before we utter a word, You know what's on our hearts. Your love is unending, and Your attention to our prayers is unwavering. Guide me, Heavenly Father, to embrace the power of prayer. Help me to trust that You hear me, even when I struggle to find the right words. May my conversations with You deepen my relationship with You, drawing me closer to Your heart. As I navigate life's complexities, may the knowledge of Your attentive ear give me peace. With a heart full of gratitude, I bring my joys, concerns, and longings to You, knowing that You are listening and responding according to Your perfect plan. In Jesus' Precious and Holy Name. Amen.

Chapter Sixteen

I KNOW that I AM

Supernaturally Blessed

~ Ephesians 1:3

In a world that often chases after material wealth, a transformative truth emerges: we are supernaturally blessed. Ephesians 1:3 declares, "Praise be to the God and Father of our Lord Jesus Christ, who has blessed us in the heavenly realms with every spiritual blessing in Christ." This chapter invites you to delve into the profound significance of supernatural blessings, supported by Scriptures that unveil the depth of our identity as recipients of divine favor and abundance.

Ephesians 1:3 magnifies the abundance we have in Jesus Christ: "Praise be to the God and Father of our Lord Jesus Christ, who has blessed us in the heavenly realms with every spiritual blessing in Christ." This verse affirms that our blessings aren't limited to the physical realm; they extend to the heavenly realms. Every spiritual blessing is ours in Jesus Christ—a treasure trove of divine provisions that transcend earthly limitations.

Galatians 3:29 speaks of our inheritance of blessings: "If you belong to Jesus Christ, then you are Abraham's seed, and heirs according to the promise." As children of God through Christ, we are heirs of God's promises. Our inheritance isn't restricted to the temporal; it includes the abundance of blessings that God has prepared for His children.

Ephesians 2:7 speaks of the riches of God's grace: "In order that in the coming ages he might show the incomparable riches of his grace, expressed in his kindness to us in Christ Jesus." The blessings we receive aren't mere tokens; they reflect the immeasurable riches of God's grace. Our lives are marked by His kindness and favor, unveiling the lavishness of His love.

Philippians 4:19 assures us of divine supply: "And my God will meet all your needs according to the riches of his glory in Christ Jesus." Our supernatural blessings aren't limited by scarcity; they are supplied according to God's boundless riches. We tap into a source of provision that exceeds human limitations and meets every need.

In conclusion, Ephesians 1:3 resounds as a declaration of our identity as supernaturally blessed individuals. Our blessings go beyond the confines of earthly wealth; they extend to the realm of spiritual treasures that define our true abundance.

As we navigate life's journey, let us live in the assurance of our supernatural blessings. Let us walk with gratitude for the riches of grace, inheritance, and divine supply that are ours in Christ. May this truth empower us to live with open hearts, ready to receive and share the abundance of blessings that flow from the heart of our gracious and loving Father.

Have there been times in your life when you felt blessed, perhaps someone gave you something that you wanted but did not ask for? Or perhaps, you were unexpectedly promoted, or someone paid for your ticket? _____
_____

Can you think of any miracles that you have witnessed in your life, or in someone elses?

_____
_____
_____

What are some of the blessings you have received that cannot be seen, but are none the less been a reality in your life? _____
_____
_____

Something to think about:

Sometimes our misfortunes turn out to be a blessing.

Dear Heavenly Father,

I come before You to offer my thanks for the abundance of supernatural blessings You've poured into my life through Jesus Christ. Your blessings go beyond the natural realm, transcending circumstances and limitations, and I am humbled by Your generosity. Thank You for the gift of salvation through Your Son, Jesus. Through His sacrifice, I am reconciled to You, forgiven, and made new. I'm in awe of the unmerited favor You've bestowed upon me, allowing me to experience Your grace, mercy, and unconditional love. Father, I'm grateful for the Holy Spirit's presence in my life. Your Holy Spirit empowers me, guides me, and fills me with supernatural wisdom and discernment. In times of weakness, Your Spirit strengthens me, reminding me that I can do all things through Christ who strengthens me. Thank You for the promises in Your Word that assure me of Your provision, protection, and guidance. You go before me and make a way even in the midst of challenges. Your supernatural blessings extend to my relationships, my health, my endeavors, and every aspect of my existence. As I reflect on the supernatural blessings I've received, may my heart be continually filled with awe and wonder. Help me to live a life that honors You, a life that radiates the blessings I've received to those around me. I commit to walking in faith, embracing the supernatural work You're doing in my life. With each step I take, may Your name be glorified, and may I reflect the light of Your supernatural blessings to a world in need. In the Mighty, Precious and Holy name of Jesus. Amen.

Image By https://stock.adobe.com/contributor/205152658/pronoia?load_type=author&prev_url=detail

Chapter Seventeen

I KNOW that I AM

Strong

~ Philippians 4:13

In a world that often magnifies weakness, a resolute truth emerges: we are strong. Philippians 4:13 proclaims, "I can do all this through him who gives me strength." This chapter invites you to explore the profound significance of our strength in Christ, supported by Scriptures that illuminate the depth of our identity as empowered and resilient individuals.

Philippians 4:13 asserts our unlimited strength in Christ: "I can do all this through him who gives me strength." This verse resonates as an empowering declaration that our strength isn't confined by our own abilities. In Christ, we possess the capacity to overcome challenges, achieve goals, and endure trials with unwavering resolve.

2 Corinthians 12:9-10 speaks of strength in weakness: "But he said to me, 'My grace is sufficient for you, for my power is made perfect in weakness.' Therefore, I will boast all the more gladly about my weaknesses, so that Christ's power may rest on me." Our weakness is not a hindrance; it's an opportunity for Christ's power to shine. When we acknowledge our vulnerability, Christ's strength becomes our foundation.

Ephesians 3:16 speaks of empowerment through the Holy Spirit: "I pray that out of his glorious riches he may strengthen you with power through his Spirit in your inner being." Our strength doesn't rely solely on our physical prowess; it's fortified by the indwelling Holy Spirit. His power operates within us, bolstering our resilience and determination.

1 John 5:4-5 speaks of victorious strength: "for everyone born of God overcomes the world. This is the victory that has overcome the world, even our faith. Who is it that overcomes the world? Only the one who believes that Jesus is the Son of God." Our strength is not just for personal triumph; it enables us to overcome the challenges and temptations of the world through our faith in Christ.

In conclusion, Philippians 4:13 resounds as a declaration of our identity as individuals who possess unwavering strength in Christ. This strength isn't self-generated; it's a divine gift that propels us beyond our limitations.

As we journey through life, let us walk in the empowerment of our strength. Let us embrace challenges with the assurance that Christ's power sustains us. May this truth inspire us to stand firm, to persevere, and to navigate life's twists and turns with unshakable confidence in the strength that Christ imparts.

Looking back, when have there been times in your life when you have done something you never dreamed you could have done? _____

_____

Do you think this could have happened without God's help? How did God help you? _____

_____

_____

In what ways has God been your strength? _____

_____

_____

Something to think about:

If God is our strength when we are weak, then what are our limitations? With God, ALL things are possible.

Dear Heavenly Father,

Your strength is my refuge in times of weakness, my rock amid challenges, and my source of unwavering courage. Thank You, Father, for empowering me beyond my own limitations. In moments when I felt overwhelmed, You carried me. In times when I doubted, Your strength became my confidence. Your presence, like a mighty fortress, surrounds me and lifts me up. Father, I recognize that the strength I have is not my own; it's a gift from You. You equip me with resilience and fortitude, allowing me to face adversity with unwavering faith. Your strength sustains me through trials and fuels my perseverance. As I journey through life, may Your strength continue to be my anchor. Help me to rely on You completely, knowing that Your power is made perfect in my weakness. Guide me to use the strength You provide to make a positive impact on the world around me. I pray that my life will reflect Your strength to others, serving as a testimony to Your faithfulness. With every step I take, may Your strength be my guiding light, leading me in paths of righteousness, and may my faith hold fast to the anchor of Your strength. In Jesus' Precious and Holy Name. Amen.

Image By Kevin Carden https://stock.adobe.com/contributor/202915633/kevin-carden?load_type=author&prev_url=detail

"Which hope we have as an anchor of the soul, both sure and stedfast…."

~ Hebrews 6:19

Chapter Eighteen

I KNOW that I AM

Complete

~ Colossians 2:10

In a world that often leaves us feeling incomplete, a transformative truth emerges: we are complete. Colossians 2:10 declares, "And in Christ you have been brought to fullness." This chapter invites you to delve into the profound significance of completeness in Christ, supported by Scriptures that illuminate the depth of our identity as individuals who lack nothing.

Colossians 2:10 affirms our fulfillment in Christ: "And in Christ you have been brought to fullness." This verse resonates as a declaration that our completeness isn't based on external factors or achievements; it's found in Christ alone. Our identity is not shaped by what we lack, but by the abundant fullness we have in Him.

Psalm 103:2-3 speaks of God's healing and wholeness: "Praise the Lord, my soul, and forget not all his benefits—who forgives all your sins and heals all your diseases." God's healing extends to both our physical and spiritual well-being. His restoration encompasses every aspect of our lives, making us whole in body and soul.

1 John 4:18 highlights the completeness found in perfect love: "There is no fear in love. But perfect love drives out fear, because fear has to do with punishment. The one who fears is not made perfect in love." God's perfect love dispels our anxieties and insecurities, filling the gaps within us with His assurance and peace.

John 10:10 speaks of abundant life in Christ: "The thief comes only to steal and kill and destroy; I have come that they may have life, and have it to the full." Christ's purpose is to bring us life in all its fullness. Our completeness isn't found in striving or accumulating, but in receiving the abundant life He offers.

In conclusion, Colossians 2:10 resounds as a proclamation of our identity as individuals who are complete in Christ. Our lives are not characterized by lack or insufficiency; they are marked by the abundant fullness that Christ bestows.

As we navigate life's journey, let us live in the assurance of our completeness. Let us embrace our identity as individuals who lack nothing in Christ. May this truth empower us to live with confidence, contentment, and the joy that comes from knowing that in Him, we are whole and complete.

Being complete means that we lack nothing. In what ways were you lacking before God made you complete?
_____

_____

In what ways has God made you complete? _____

_____

_____

When you have a task to complete, do you have to work to complete it? What work has God done for you to be made whole and complete? _____

_____

_____

Something to think about:

To be complete is also to be confident and content. To be confident and content is not to become stagnant, but to be free and inspired to do. Many good things come from being confident and content.

Dear Heavenly Father,

I thank You for the completeness I find in You alone. Your presence fills every space, bringing harmony and contentment. You are my source of strength and satisfaction. I praise You for the way You make me whole, providing everything I need. In Your completeness, I find peace and purpose. Thank You for the complete and abundant life You have given me. In Jesus' Precious and Holy Name. Amen.

nwww.freepik.com Image By freepik

"And to know the love of Christ, which passeth knowledge, that ye might be filled with all the fullness of God."

~ Ephesians 3:19

Chapter Nineteen

I KNOW that I AM

More than A Conqueror

~ Romans 6:4

In a world filled with challenges and uncertainties, a triumphant truth emerges: we are more than conquerors. Romans 8:37 proclaims, "No, in all these things we are more than conquerors through him who loved us." This chapter invites you to explore the profound significance of being more than conquerors, supported by Scriptures that illuminate the depth of our identity as individuals who overcome through Christ's love.

Romans 8:37 proclaims our status as triumphant conquerors: "No, in all these things we are more than conquerors through him who loved us." This verse resonates as a declaration of our victory over trials, tribulations, and challenges that we face. Our triumph doesn't merely result in survival; it encompasses a resounding victory through Christ's love.

1 John 5:4 speaks of overcoming the world through faith: "for everyone born of God overcomes the world. This is the victory that has overcome the world, even our faith." Our faith in Christ is the foundation of our victory. By being born of God, we have the capacity to overcome the world's influences and temptations.

Philippians 4:13 asserts our strength in Christ's power: "I can do all this through him who gives me strength." The strength that enables us to conquer doesn't come from our own abilities, but from Christ's empowerment. His strength empowers us to face challenges and emerge victorious.

James 1:12 speaks of the reward for those who endure trials: "Blessed is the one who perseveres under trial because, having stood the test, that person will receive the crown of life that the Lord has promised to those who love him." Our identity as conquerors involves persevering through trials with a heart devoted to Christ, leading to a promised reward.

In conclusion, Romans 8:37 resounds as a proclamation of our identity as individuals who are more than conquerors. Our triumphs extend beyond momentary victories; they reflect an enduring, Christ-fueled victory over life's challenges.

As we journey through life, let us live in the assurance of being more than conquerors. Let us face trials with unwavering faith, knowing that Christ's love and power enable us to emerge victorious. May this truth empower us to navigate life with confidence, resilience, and a spirit that reflects the triumphant identity we have in Christ.

How many times in life have you had to overcome a challenge or a trial? _____

_____

Did your faith help you overcome it? _____   In what way? _____

_____

_____

We all endure trials and tribulations in life. We know that they will come. How do we know that we can overcome them, and how does that impact our lives? _____

_____

_____

In what way are you more than a conqueror? _____

_____

_____

Something to think about:

A conqueror overcomes his enemy. One who is more than a conqueror, not only overcomes his enemy, but makes his enemy his servant. When Jesus said "pray for your enemies', He was teaching us to be more than a conqueror.

Dear Heavenly Father,

I come before You with a heart full of gratitude for the promise that I am more than a conqueror through Christ Jesus. Your Word assures me that no challenge, trial, or obstacle can separate me from Your love and victory. Thank You for the strength and courage You instill in me, allowing me to rise above circumstances that may try to defeat me. I embrace the truth that Your power within me is greater than any force against me. Father, help me to walk in the confidence of being more than a conqueror. Let this truth permeate my thoughts and actions, reminding me that I am equipped to overcome every challenge that comes my way. Grant me the wisdom to see beyond the temporary struggles, knowing that Your ultimate victory has already been secured. May I live each day with resilience and unwavering faith in You. As I face trials, may Your presence be my fortress and Your love my shield. Let me stand strong, knowing that Your strength empowers me to conquer and overcome. Thank You, Heavenly Father, for making me more than a conqueror through the love of my Redeemer, Jesus Christ. With every step I take, may Your victory shine through me, and may I reflect Your glory to the world around me. Let me remember in all things, especially when this world is cruel, that You have overcame the world. Thank You Father. In Jesus' Precious and Holy Name. Amen.

Chapter Twenty

I KNOW that I AM

Kept

~ 1 Peter 1:5

In a world marked by uncertainty, a comforting truth emerges: we are kept. 1 Peter 1:5 affirms, "who through faith are shielded by God's power until the coming of the salvation that is ready to be revealed in the last time." This chapter invites you to explore the profound significance of being securely kept by God, supported by Scriptures that illuminate the depth of our identity as individuals who are under His protective care.

1 Peter 1:5 assures us of being shielded by God's power: "who through faith are shielded by God's power until the coming of the salvation that is ready to be revealed in the last time." This verse resonates as a declaration that our security doesn't rest in our own efforts, but in God's unfailing power. His protective shield encompasses us, guarding us through every season of life.

John 10:28-29 speaks of our security in the Shepherd's care: "I give them eternal life, and they shall never perish; no one will snatch them out of my hand. My Father, who has given them to me, is greater than all; no one can snatch them out of my Father's hand." Our safekeeping isn't vulnerable to external threats; we are held securely in the hands of the Shepherd and the Father.

Psalm 121:7-8 speaks of God's preservation in times of trial: "The Lord will keep you from all harm—he will watch over your life; the Lord will watch over your coming and going both now and forevermore." Our security extends to every aspect of our lives—present and future. In times of adversity, God's watchful care ensures our preservation.

2 Thessalonians 3:3 underscores God's faithfulness in keeping us: "But the Lord is faithful, and he will strengthen you and protect you from the evil one." God's faithfulness is a guarantee of our protection. He strengthens us and guards us from the schemes of the enemy, ensuring our well-being.

In conclusion, 1 Peter 1:5 resounds as a declaration of our identity as individuals who are securely kept by God. Our safety is not contingent on circumstances; it's anchored in His unwavering faithfulness.

As we navigate life's uncertainties, let us live in the assurance of being kept. Let us rest in the knowledge that God's protective power shields us from harm. May this truth empower us to live with confidence, courage, and a deep sense of peace, knowing that we are under the constant, loving care of our Heavenly Father.

In what ways are you kept by God? _____

_____

_____

What is the result of knowing that you are kept by God? _____

_____

_____

How does it change how you see your future? _____

_____

_____

Something to think about:

The word 'kept' is past tense. We are kept by God and He will continue keeping us safe. But we are 'kept' because by His power it is already done. When Jesus said on the cross "It is finished", it was finished. When we were saved, we became kept. God has provided everything needed for us to be safe and provided for. It is more than just keeping us, it is a safe haven where we are kept. No matter what our futures hold, as far as our safety and needs, God declares it is done.

Dear Heavenly Father,

I humbly come before You with a heart full of gratitude for Your faithful keeping. Thank You for being my refuge, my shelter, and my safe haven. In times of uncertainty, You are my constant solidarity and my fortress. I am grateful, Father, that Your arms of protection are always around me. Your love surrounds me like a strong tower, shielding me from harm. Thank You for being my security in every season of life. Father, I find comfort in knowing that You are my eternal safe haven. Amid life's storms, I can rest in Your unchanging presence. You are my anchor, and I trust in Your unwavering love and care. As I journey through each day, may I continue to find solace in Your embrace. Help me to lean on You and to seek refuge in Your promises. Your faithfulness is my assurance, and Your presence is my peace. Be forever present with me Father. I know that nothing will snatch me from Your hand or from the hand of my beloved redeemer, Jesus Christ. Thank You, Heavenly Father, for keeping me close to Your heart. In every moment, I am held by Your loving hands. I entrust myself to Your care and protection, now and forevermore. In Jesus' Precious and Holy Name. Amen.

Chapter Twenty-One

I KNOW that I AM

Inseparable

~ Romans 8:38-39

In a world where relationships can falter, a profound truth emerges: we are inseparable from God's love. Romans 8:38-39 declares, "For I am convinced that neither death nor life, neither angels nor demons, neither the present nor the future, nor any powers, neither height nor depth, nor anything else in all creation, will be able to separate us from the love of God that is in Christ Jesus our Lord." This chapter invites you to delve into the profound significance of being inseparable from God's love, supported by Scriptures that illuminate the depth of our identity as individuals bound eternally to Him.

Romans 8:38-39 affirms our unbreakable bond with God's love: "For I am convinced that neither death nor life, neither angels nor demons, neither the present nor the future, nor any powers, neither height nor depth, nor anything else in all creation, will be able to separate us from the love of God that is in Christ Jesus our Lord." This passage resounds as a declaration that our connection with God's love is beyond the reach of any force, circumstance, or entity. Our unity with Him endures, unbreakable and eternal.

John 10:28-29 speaks of our eternal security in Christ's hand: "I give them eternal life, and they shall never perish; no one will snatch them out of my hand. My Father, who has given them to me, is greater than all; no one can snatch them out of my Father's hand." Our position in Christ's hand isn't subject to being plucked away. It's an everlasting bond that cannot be severed.

Hebrews 13:5 emphasizes God's faithful commitment: "Never will I leave you; never will I forsake you." Our inseparability from God isn't based on our merit, but on His unwavering promise. He remains steadfast in His commitment to be with us through every moment of our lives.

1 John 5:13 assures us of eternal life in Christ: "I write these things to you who believe in the name of the Son of God so that you may know that you have eternal life." Our inseparability from God's love is firmly grounded in our faith in Christ. This assurance enables us to live with confidence and hope.

In conclusion, the profound truth of Romans 8:38-39 resounds as a proclamation of our identity as individuals inseparably bound to God's love. Our connection with Him transcends time, circumstances, and powers.

As we journey through life's uncertainties, let us live in the assurance of our inseparability. Let us face challenges with unwavering faith, knowing that we are forever linked to the One who loves us without reservation. May this truth empower us to live with courage, perseverance, and a profound sense of peace, rooted in our unbreakable bond with the God who loves us beyond measure.

Have there been times in your life that you did not feel loved? _____

Have there been times in your life when you felt abandoned and alone? _____

Even though you felt that way, your feelings did not match the truth that God has spoken. So, even though those feelings were real, were they true? _____

Where do you think those feelings came from? _____

If in the future, there is a time that you feel alone, abandoned or unloved, how will handle it?

_____

_____

_____

Something to think about:

God's love is the highest and greatest power to exist, and He has given it to YOU. He promised to never leave you or forsake you. That means He is with you, right here, right now and in every moment from the past to eternity.

Dear Heavenly Father,

I come before You with a heart full of gratitude for the promise that nothing can separate me from Your love. Your Word assures me that I am held securely in Your embrace, and I find comfort in knowing that I am inseparable from Your presence. Thank You for the assurance that neither height nor depth, nor any other created thing, seen or unseen, can separate me from Your unfailing love. Your bond with me is unshakable and unbreakable, and I rest in the certainty and steadfast faith, that Your love and faithfulness endures forever. Father, help me to live each day with the confidence that I am forever united with You. May this truth shape my perspective and my life, giving me courage to face challenges and grace to overcome them. Your presence empowers me to navigate life's journey. As I walk this path, may Your inseparable love be a guiding light. May it strengthen my faith, ignite my hope, and inspire my actions. Let my life be pleasing to You and a testimony to the unbreakable bond I share with You. Thank You, Heavenly Father, for the gift of being inseparable from Your love. In every moment, I am held close by Your eternal embrace. I trust in Your faithfulness and stand firm in Your unchanging promise. In Jesus' Precious and Holy Name. Amen.

Chapter Twenty-Two

I KNOW

The Great I AM

~ John 8:58

As we journeyed through these chapters, a resounding truth emerged: the more intimately we know God, the more profoundly we understand ourselves. These chapters, each rooted in a distinct aspect of our identity in Christ, collectively unveil the intricate tapestry of who we are when embraced by His love, grace, and purpose. From being cherished above all to being kept and inseparable, we witness a harmonious melody—a symphony of truths that resound in the depths of our souls.

Through the chapters, we've come to grasp that in knowing God's unbreakable love, we discover our inseparability from Him. In understanding His sovereign power, we uncover our security and completion. His grace reveals our redemption, and His faithfulness mirrors our identity as conquerors. This journey unveiled not only our identity but also the journey toward becoming the best version of ourselves.

Our reflection in God's truth is akin to gazing into a mirror, one that doesn't distort but illuminates. As we seek Him, we become aware of our uniqueness and purpose—a purpose interwoven with His grand design. The more we delve into His character, the more we unearth the facets of our own. Just as a diamond's brilliance is uncovered as it's polished, our true brilliance shines as we allow God's truth to refine us.

In essence, the journey of self-discovery is intertwined with our pursuit of knowing God. We are a masterpiece painted on the canvas of His boundless love, shaped by His hands of purpose. As we venture deeper into His truth, we uncover the intricacies of our own story—layer by layer, truth by truth. It's a journey where self-revelation aligns with our relationship with Him, where our identity blossoms like a flower unfolding in the warmth of His presence.

May we hold onto this profound revelation: that in the depths of knowing God, we find the keys to understanding ourselves. Let our hearts remain open to the transformative journey, one that continually unravels the beauty of our identity while unveiling the splendor of our Creator. In the dance of self-discovery and God's revelation, we truly become who we were always meant to be—mirrors reflecting His glory, love, and purpose.

What have you learned about God? _____

_____

_____

What have you learned about yourself? _____

_____

_____

How has this helped you in moving forward into your future? _____

_____

_____

What views or ideas did you have before, that have now changed? _____

_____

_____

Something to think about:

If you do not like yourself, don't blame God, but thank God, because He is bringing you to the point where you realize that you need Him. And the truth is, if you don't like yourself, then you are not seeing God, or who God made you to be, which means the best is yet to come!

Dear Heavenly Father,

With a heart brimming with gratitude, I thank You for the incredible journey of faith You've led me on. Thank You for every step, every twist and turn, for being with me through it all. Your presence has been my constant companion, guiding me, comforting me, and lifting me up. I am filled with gratitude for all the lessons You've graciously taught me. Thank You for revealing Yourself to me, for showing me the depths of Your love and the beauty of Your salvation. I am humbled by Your patient guidance and unwavering presence. Father, I cherish the knowledge You've bestowed upon me. Through Your Word, through experiences, and through moments of revelation, You have led me into a deeper understanding of who You are. Thank You for unveiling the truths that bring me closer to Your heart. Father, I am thankful that You hear me, even when my words fail me. Your attentiveness to my prayers reminds me of Your unwavering love and care. Thank You for knowing the depths of my heart and meeting me right where I am. I praise You for making me a cherished part of Your royal family. Through the sacrifice of Your Son, I am now a co-heir with Christ, blessed with Your eternal inheritance. You've made my identity secure in You, and I find my worth in being Your child. Thank You Father, for the unique gifts and talents You've bestowed upon me. You've fashioned me with purpose, and I'm grateful for the opportunity to use my uniqueness to bring glory to Your name. I pray, Father, that our relationship continues to grow stronger and closer in the future and always. May our connection deepen as I seek Your face, lean on Your wisdom, and align my heart with Your will. Help me to hunger for Your presence more each day. As I journey forward, may I walk in the light of Your teachings. Strengthen my faith, refine my character, and draw me into a closer intimacy with You. May my life reflect the transformation that comes from knowing You deeply. Father, my heart longs for the day when I will see You face to face. The hope of that glorious encounter fills me with anticipation and joy. Until then, may my life be a reflection of Your love and grace, a testimony to the transformation that comes from knowing You intimately. I am forever thankful for this journey, for Your presence, and for the bright future You have prepared for me. In Jesus' Precious and Holy Name. Amen.

Image by Rafael https://stock.adobe.com/contributor/211276710/rafael?load_type=author&prev_url=detail

" Go ye therefore, and teach all nations, baptizing them in the name of the Father, and of the Son, and of the Holy Ghost: Teaching them to observe all things whatsoever I have commanded you: and, lo, I am with you always, even unto the end of the world. Amen."

~ Matthew 28:19-20

"He which testifieth these things saith, Surely, I come quickly. Amen. Even so, come, Lord Jesus. The grace of our Lord Jesus Christ be with you all. Amen"

~ Revelation 22:20-21

Chapter Twenty-Three

I KNOW that I AM

His Story

~ Revelations 22:13

Through these scriptures God has revealed Himself and has reminded us chapter by chapter of who we are. To put it simply in a letter, this is what God wants to remind you.

My Dear Beloved, (introduction)

I want to remind you of who you are to Me. I made you in My Image (chapter one), not because I AM perfect, but because I want all perfect things for you. I treasure you, above all my creation (chapter two). I have always known you, from the time I purposed you in My heart, before I formed you in your mother's womb, I knew everything about you, all the good that you would think and do throughout your entire life on earth, as well as all the bad. I knew the end from the beginning, before you were created, but I loved you and created you anyway. You began from my heart, and I created you for a purpose; because it pleased Me to love you. (chapter three). You are very precious to Me, and I love you more than you could ever fathom (chapter four). I created you just the way you are and gave you every ability to prosper, I even commanded that you go forth and multiply. I created all the earth, and the whole universe to be yours, to watch you grow and prosper, to watch all the beauty that I created become more beautiful with you prospering in it (chapter five). I have always been there with you watching you grow, and you have been my joy and my delight (chapter six). I want you to know that I chose you and I long for you to choose Me. I gave you free will, to choose Me or not, because I want your true love in return. You have the choice in every moment of every day to choose me or to choose yourself and the world, and I know sometimes you don't know what you want, but I want you to know that I do not change. I am a constant in your life, whether you realize it or not, I am always looking out for you, but never trespassing against your wishes. When I chose you, I meant it (chapter seven). I was and I am deadly serious about you, and I won't change my mind. But it's up to you to choose me. I made a way to bring your heart back to me and be reconciled with me. I came to where you are on earth, and I took upon myself the punishment of your sins to save you from the curse of death so that you could live with me and so we could be together every day for all eternity. I have saved you from the curse, but you must believe that and trust me. Ultimately, it is up to you to accept my sacrifice for you. I died and defeated the curse of death and hell for your sins, because I want you to live (chapter eight). I want you to live and be free. When you were born into the world, you were born into sin with the curse of death engulfing you all around. You have seen it all around you from the time you were too little to understand. But that is never what I wanted for you, sin was never a part of my plan, but my enemy and your enemy's plan to steal, kill and destroy you. You will die. But when you accept that I died on the cross to pay the penalty for your sin, from that very moment when you accept Me into your heart and ask Me to be Lord of your life, all of heaven rejoices because from that moment, you are a new person (chapter 9), the person I created you to be, and though your body may die, I will raise it up again. You are redeemed from the grave and will live for all eternity with me in heaven and on earth. For the rest of your days on earth, My Spirit will live with you. You will come to know Me, more and more, as our relationship grows. You will see things differently, I will show you and teach you things, even Heavenly things, and you will live a new life as a citizen of My Kingdom (Chapter 10). Not only will you be a citizen, but you, my beloved, are my child, and a royal heir to My very throne (chapter 11). I and the Father are One. I am the King of Kings and Lord of Lords and sit at the right hand of the Father. When you accept Me and My Spirit dwells in you, we are one as I prayed in John 17. You become a member of My Body (chapter 12), and a rightful heir of all that is Mine on Heaven and Earth. When you accepted Me, My blood covered you so that the Father could accept you. You are accepted (chapter 13). You can come to me as you are, not in false pretense. Come to me in all your brokenness and I will accept you and make you whole again. My love has covered all that is unacceptable, and My blood has made you clean (chapter 14). I have heard your souls cry, even when you haven't been able to speak or think, I hear you (chapter 15), I have always and will always listen with compassion and understanding. I want you to know how blessed you are. Not only will I meet your every need on earth, but I have given you blessings in the heavenly realms, and one day you will see and understand. You may not realize it, but you are storing up treasures in Heaven and there is so much more that waits for you there (chapter 16). So be strong and endure. You are stronger than you think through Me, because when you are weak, I will be your strength (chapter 17), I will carry you through. In Me, you are complete (chapter 18), and you are more than a conqueror. With Me, there is nothing impossible, nothing you cannot accomplish, nothing that you cannot endure. Be strong and of good courage, I will help you and when you ask me, I will answer. When the world hates you, remember it hated Me first, and My victory over the world is also your victory. I overcame the world and have called you out of it and you have been given the power of My Holy Spirit to work through you. It is the power that resurrected me from the grave, the same power that has led you to me, and the power that will help you and one day bring you forth from the grave and back home to Me. You are more than a conqueror through Me (chapter 19). Until then, I will keep you, and I have kept you from the beginning (chapter 20). I will strengthen you. I will protect you from the enemy. I want you to trust and obey me. I will be your shield and give you life everlasting, and nothing and no one will pluck you out of my hand. I am yours and you are Mine. I love you and I AM with you always, even until the end of the ages (chapter 21).

Love eternally,

The Great "I AM"

Image by Canva.com

John 17 (KJV)

1 These words spake Jesus, and lifted up his eyes to heaven, and said, Father, the hour is come; glorify thy Son, that thy Son also may glorify thee:

2 As thou hast given him power over all flesh, that he should give eternal life to as many as thou hast given him.

3 And this is life eternal, that they might know thee the only true God, and Jesus Christ, whom thou hast sent.

4 I have glorified thee on the earth: I have finished the work which thou gavest me to do.

5 And now, O Father, glorify thou me with thine own self with the glory which I had with thee before the world was.

6 I have manifested thy name unto the men which thou gavest me out of the world: thine they were, and thou gavest them me; and they have kept thy word.

7 Now they have known that all things whatsoever thou hast given me are of thee.

8 For I have given unto them the words which thou gavest me; and they have received them, and have known surely that I came out from thee, and they have believed that thou didst send me.

9 I pray for them: I pray not for the world, but for them which thou hast given me; for they are thine.

10 And all mine are thine, and thine are mine; and I am glorified in them.

11 And now I am no more in the world, but these are in the world, and I come to thee. Holy Father, keep through thine own name those whom thou hast given me, that they may be one, as we are.

12 While I was with them in the world, I kept them in thy name: those that thou gavest me I have kept, and none of them is lost, but the son of perdition; that the scripture might be fulfilled.

13 And now come I to thee; and these things I speak in the world, that they might have my joy fulfilled in themselves.

14 I have given them thy word; and the world hath hated them, because they are not of the world, even as I am not of the world.

15 I pray not that thou shouldest take them out of the world, but that thou shouldest keep them from the evil.

16 They are not of the world, even as I am not of the world.

17 Sanctify them through thy truth: thy word is truth.

18 As thou hast sent me into the world, even so have I also sent them into the world.

19 And for their sakes I sanctify myself, that they also might be sanctified through the truth.

20 Neither pray I for these alone, but for them also which shall believe on me through their word;

21 That they all may be one; as thou, Father, art in me, and I in thee, that they also may be one in us: that the world may believe that thou hast sent me.

22 And the glory which thou gavest me I have given them; that they may be one, even as we are one:

23 I in them, and thou in me, that they may be made perfect in one; and that the world may know that thou hast sent me, and hast loved them, as thou hast loved me.

24 Father, I will that they also, whom thou hast given me, be with me where I am; that they may behold my glory, which thou hast given me: for thou lovedst me before the foundation of the world.

25 O righteous Father, the world hath not known thee: but I have known thee, and these have known that thou hast sent me.

26 And I have declared unto them thy name and will declare it: that the love wherewith thou hast loved me may be in them, and I in them.

References

The Holy Bible. Authorized King James Version, Thomas Nelson Publishers, 1990

Open AI. ChatGPT – Language Models. URL: https://openai.com/research/models Accessed 2023

Images, pg. 12, 21, 39, 48, 61   https://freepik.com

Images, pg. 29, 35, 54, 58, 74   https://stock.adobe.com

Image, pg. 77, 81   https://canva.com

Image by https://canva.com

Made in the USA
Columbia, SC
22 January 2024